Essential Skills for Hackers

Essential Skills for Hackers

Kevin Cardwell

Contributing Editor
Henry Dalziel

ELSEVIER

AMSTERDAM • BOSTON • HEIDELBERG • LONDON
NEW YORK • OXFORD • PARIS • SAN DIEGO
SAN FRANCISCO • SINGAPORE • SYDNEY • TOKYO

Syngress is an imprint of Elsevier

SYNGRESS.

Syngress is an imprint of Elsevier
225 Wyman Street, Waltham, MA 02451, USA

Notices
Knowledge and best practice in this field are constantly changing. As new research and experience broaden our understanding, changes in research methods or professional practices, may become necessary.

Practitioners and researchers must always rely on their own experience and knowledge in evaluating and using any information or methods described herein. In using such information or methods they should be mindful of their own safety and the safety of others, including parties for whom they have a professional responsibility.

To the fullest extent of the law, neither the Publisher nor the authors, contributors, or editors, assume any liability for any injury and/or damage to persons or property as a matter of products liability, negligence or otherwise, or from any use or operation of any methods, products, instructions, or ideas contained in the material herein.

ISBN: 978-0-12-804755-2

British Library Cataloguing-in-Publication Data
A catalogue record for this book is available from the British Library

Library of Congress Cataloging-in-Publication Data
A catalog record for this book is available from the Library of Congress

For Information on all Syngress publications
visit our website at http://store.elsevier.com/Syngress

This book has been manufactured using Print On Demand technology.

CONTENTS

ABOUT THE AUTHORS

Henry Dalziel is a serial education entrepreneur, founder of Concise Ac Ltd, online cybersecurity blogger, and e-book author. He writes for the Concise-Courses.com blog and has developed numerous cybersecurity continuing education courses and books. Concise Ac Ltd develops and distributes continuing education content [books and courses] for cybersecurity professionals seeking skill enhancement and career advancement. The company was recently accepted onto the UK Trade & Investment's (UKTI) Global Entrepreneur Programme (GEP).

Kevin Cardwell works as a freelance consultant and provides consulting services for companies throughout the world, and as an advisor to numerous government entities within the US, Middle East, Africa, Asia, and the UK. He is an Instructor, Technical Editor and Author for Computer Forensics, and Hacking courses. He is author of Building Virtual Pentesting Labs for Advanced Penetration Testing. Currently providing consultancy to ASM on curriculum development and information security projects in security for Government clients within the US.

INTRODUCTION

Essential Skills for Hackers is about the skills you need to be in the elite hacker.

Some people, when they actually go and try to hack, think of it in terms of what they see in an application. What we want to do as hackers and, more importantly, as security professionals however is to be able to look at different layers of the model and understand it at the lower layers, the physical layer.

We're talking about the open system interconnect OSI model, which we'll cover. What that model does is it allows us to break down each functionality of the network from the time it becomes bits of either voltage or light depending on if you're in fiber or on copper, and then as it goes up through the process until it gets to the application layer that the user sees.

I want to talk mainly about two things: TCP/IP 101. That is we want to understand: TCP/IP, as well as the alphabet. This is very important when it comes to hacking because everything we're going to do, unless we physically sit down on the machine, is going to require network traffic. So the better the hacker, the more we will be able to master TCP/IP.

And then we're going to talk about protocol analysis. Once we understand what TCP/IP is, what it looks like, we're going to go into protocol analysis and how analyzing the protocol or, in a more general sense, looking at packets on the wire, we will be able to determine what exactly is taking place on a network. By doing this, we can identify when something on the network doesn't match what it should and, more importantly, we can create any type of sequence of events or packets that we want on the network and see how the defenses or the machines that we send them to react. And that's the power of doing TCP/IP protocol analysis. So let's go ahead and get started.

CHAPTER 1

Network Protocols

Chapter Objectives

- Review Network Protocols
- Examine Packet Headers
- Analyze Traffic

TCP/IP 101:

We're going to look at network protocols; that is, the different network protocols that we have out there. The two main ones are what we have been saying is TCP/IP. We'll discuss IP, ICMP, and some different types of protocols. Then, we're going to look at actual packet headers. Because what happens is every piece of data as it transits a different layer of the OSI model will have a header added to it. By understanding these headers, we can understand what is taking place in the sequence of events and on the network. That is very important when we're going to do this, so we understand how the packets are being routed up the stack and down the stack. And then we're going to analyze traffic and we're going to talk about the process of traffic analysis.

What we mean by that is we're going to actually look at the packets and analyze what's taking place. We're going to look at normal activity, so we understand what looks normal and then we're going to look at abnormal activity, so we understand what we will see if a hacker or somebody is doing some type of attack; we'll know what it looks like at the packet level. And the most important thing about understanding TCP/IP 101 is what do the packets look like when somebody is conducting one on normal traffic? What do they look like when somebody's doing abnormal or what we call "Crafted," packets? And what does it look when one of our machines gets infected with one of these well publicized attacks, be it malware, denial of service, any of those types of things? These are all the things we want to cover in this chapter.

Network Protocols

- The Internet was built on an open, standardized suite of communication protocols
- Despite technology advances, the Internet is still run by the protocols that were originally created
  - IP
  - TCP
  - UDP
- Communication between a client and a server is through *ports*
  - Clients typically operate on ports > 1023
    - ☐ *Ephemeral*
  - Servers typically operate on ports < 1023
    - ☐ *Privileged*

What are we talking about with Network Protocols? We're mainly talking about the fact that the internet was built on an open standardized suite of communication protocol. But what is a protocol? A protocol is the way something communicates and that's the easiest way to understand a protocol. It's communication. When the internet was created, they had to have some means of protocol. How do we communicate with computers from a computer to a computer, right? Even though we have had all these years of advances in the Internet, it still ran on the protocol for the original internet and that protocol is TCP/IP, created by Dr Vint Cerf and Dr Robert Khan. And what they were given was the task for the Internet, which of course was the small university and government military research network. They were given the task of giving us some form of communication that you could guarantee would be delivered, and then give us a form of communication that doesn't have the guarantee but is used for speed when speeds are concerned. So that was the main TCP/IP.

What we got is Internet Protocol or IP at the highest level, which is the main part of the packet. But the IP has what we call encapsulation. That encapsulation, which we'll get into here momentarily, is when you put things within other things. And we have two main protocols that we usually use and they are TCP, Transmission Control Protocol, and UDP, User Datagram Protocol. We will get deeper into this when we discuss ICMP, Internet Control Message.

The next part to understand is communications. When they created the internet, they knew they had to have two parties or two machines;

parties are represented in the machines and these machines have to be able to communicate. And this communication had to come across some form of a network so they had to set it up. The typical relationship of how to understand this is as a client and a server. How do the clients and the servers communicate? They need a door, right? A client needs a door where I can send something through the door to get to the server. And the server has to have a door to send it back to.

These doors are what we call ports. And ports are exactly as I said, they are doors. And the way it was set up in the original standard, which is kind of blurred today but it's still important to know, was that your clients typically operate on ports that we call greater than 1023, and that is port 1024–65,535 because we have 65,536 ports. These ports are typically where clients operate. Why do they operate there? Because we only need them in a temporary or a transient state. As clients, think about it: When you are on the Internet, what do you do? You connect, you click on a link, you're making multiple connections in a relatively short time and you're not really doing any time in that connection. So these types of connections are what we consider ephemeral and that is where ports that the clients use greater than 1023 are traditionally called ephemeral. Ephemeral means short-lived or transitory. That is exactly what we do as clients. As clients, we're only going to connect as long as we need to do things. The last research that was published said that the average time that a user spends on a website, before they move to the next site, is 4 seconds. This is the world we have come to where we are only going to be on a site a very short time. Even though when the Internet was built, it was built with very small numbers, they had the concept that clients are going to spend time connecting but not time staying connected, so we set up these ephemeral and, more importantly when we talk about HTTP, in Hypertext Transfer Protocol stateless type of connections.

The servers are different. Think about what a server does. A server sits there with services, it's designed to serve. What it is doing when it's designed to serve is it has ports or doors opened to different services that the communication protocol has to use. These servers typically run on ports less than 1023. That was until we started running out of the lower, less than 1023 ports, because we got Skype, we got Sip for voiceover IP. We have all these other protocols so it got a little bit crowded there in the port 1–1023 range. So some of those are all running at different ports above 1023 but traditionally, servers operate on ports less than 1023. If you think about web, HTTP, Hypertext Transfer Protocol, that is port 80. HTTPS, HTTP, Hypertext Transfer Protocol Secure, that is, port 443. Post Office Protocol port 110. Most of these servers and services always run on ports less than 1023 until you got later in the environment when, as I said, it became a little harder to do that. An example is Microsoft SQL, it runs on port 1433 so it's not less than 1023 and it's an actual service that runs on 1433. And then Oracle is 1521. This gives you the idea.

Anyways, we call these traditionally privileged ports. Why do we call them privileged ports? We call them privileged ports because you had to have privileged user access to be able to manipulate and access the port in the UNIX Linux world during the creation of the Internet. And then somebody got the bright idea, "No, we're not going to do all that, we're just going to go ahead and have everybody have access to ports." Well, that idea, as you can imagine, didn't go over very well and eventually they realized that was a bad idea. What happened is that, starting with Service Pack 2, Windows Service Pack 2 and beyond, they stopped giving the users access to raw sockets. What's a socket? We'll come to that here momentarily.

Transport Protocols

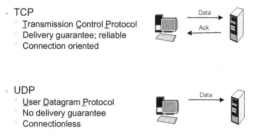

- Port numbers identify service to which data is delivered

This is what it looks like TCP, as you see in the diagram; the key here is the data always get an acknowledgment. That is why the delivery is guaranteed and it is a reliable connection oriented. It's connection oriented because it has to establish a connection before data can fly. And we'll talk about how that works as we go through the actual chapter. User Datagram Protocol, is connection less, so when you look at a diagram for User Datagram Protocol, you recognize that the data do not get an acknowledgment. When the data don't get an acknowledgment, that means it's connection less. There is no delivery guarantee. Why? It assumes the path is always there. A good indication of this is you think about how our mail system works. There is no guarantee your mail is going to get to the destination. In fact, the post office loses quite a bit of mail every year, believe it or not, but we assume that it's going to get there and we rely on another party to transport it. This is exactly what happens with UDP; we rely on the connection medium to take care of the transportation. We do a connection-less protocol. We don't want to give a three-way handshake where we have to communicate with the server back and forth to make sure the connection is there and then send the data. No, we don't want to do that. What we want to do is we want to send the data and not wait for it to be acknowledged. This is used a lot in streaming protocol and that type of stuff.

What happens when a packet gets to a machine, how does it know where to go? The port number identifies the service to where the data is going and that's how the process works. Now that's in the simplest terms. We'll talk more about this because it is not just the port number. Yes, the port number will identify the service, but we have to have a little bit more information to get the data actually into the machine in itself. And we'll talk about those concepts later on.

CHAPTER 2

Packet Headers

Headers

- Each protocol has a header corresponding to a particular layer
  - Protocols operate at a single specific layer
  - Identifies the data to the service that receives it
  - Determines protocol behavior
- It is critical to understand the structure of all relevant protocol headers
- This knowledge is essential for controlling access throughout the enterprise and is the foundation for device configuration

On to headers. As I said in the introduction, each protocol has a header that corresponds to a particular layer. They operate a specific layer. At layer 2, which is the data link layer, the data link header has the specific data it has to have for the data link layer. That identifies the data of the service that receives it and determines its behavior, what it's going to do, and the essential component of all your hacking. Security skills or whatever you're trying to do out in the industry, it's critical to understand the structure of all these protocol headers because you're going to have to read these at the packet level. At the binary level, almost anybody who's been around the field many years doesn't really want to go read binary. We'll settle for hex but we're not going to read those bits of binary one and zeroes and stuff like that. But it's important that you know this because it is essential for how we control access for our enterprise network, and it's also your foundation for how you are going to figure your devices. You have to configure the devices that support the protocols that you use. Of course, you could just say, "Well, you know what? I am going to allow everything." Promiscuous mode, which we will discuss, means that we have no address filtering on; we allow everything. There is a concern with that because the hackers have discovered that they can hack and do all of this cool stuff. So it's not the best idea to allow everything.

Headers
(continued)

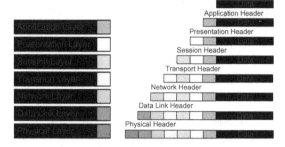

Here's what the header's look like in this diagram. You have the application layer, and it puts an application header on it. You have the presentation layer and it depends on what happens, if it goes down from you typing on your computer in that window. For example, if you're doing your Outlook or your mail, mail programs, you're doing messaging—whatever you're doing that's the application layer. As you're typing on that and you click send to send that email or you type in HTTP, www.whateverwebsite.com; when you do that, you're actually at the application layer. The first thing that happens when you hit send or when you hit enter on the enter key is that you're going to a website and it's going to go from the application layer down to the actual protocol stack. It's going to go from the application layer down to the presentation layer. Remember, we're talking the OSI model here. Then it pins, on top of the application header, the presentation header. Then it goes down to the next layer and puts on the session header. And the next layer to put the transport header, network header, data link header, and then finally it gets to the bottom, which is the physical layer with the physical header as the last layer added onto the header of the data packet. But as you see in the diagram, all seven layers have a corresponding header. So what happens is now when it hits the physical layer, it's your binary, it's your ones and zeroes. What happens from there? Well, those ones and zeroes are turned into voltage if you're using copper or pulses of light; if you're using fiber and then that is transmitted on the wire. So whatever your medium is—be it copper, we'll call it wire—that's just terminology—or if it's fiber, then it's light, of course—it's going to transmit the data in ones and zeroes to the destination. That's the process.

Encapsulation

- The process of wrapping information
  - "The inclusion of one thing within another thing so that the included thing is not apparent"*
- This is how the network traffic is composed as it transits from machine to machine
  - Each layer has a specific function from data to the wire
- By understanding the structure of network traffic, you can validate and verify what is passing through access-control devices

*Sourcewww.searchnetworking.com

This process is called encapsulation. That's the process of wrapping information. It's the inclusion of one thing within another thing so that the included thing is not apparent. That is how all your traffic can pose as it transmits from machine to machine. Each layer has a specific function from data to the wire. As we said, when you're at the application layer and you're sending the packets all the way down to the physical layer, each layer has a corresponding function that it takes control and does. Layer 3 is our routing, and that's how it finds what networks to go to. Layer 2 is our data link layer; that's how it knows its physical or MAC, media access control, address, which is how all the data are delivered. The data are delivered to the physical address. This is essential when you're going to do your devices and verify what's passing through your network. We have to understand the process.

Encapsulation (continued)

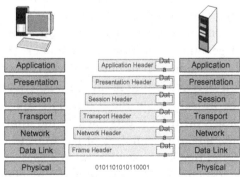

When you look at this next diagram, you see we've got the application layer, the presentation session, and transport network data link, which has a frame header, and then we have the physical layers, that's ones and zeroes. When we're at the application and we send our email and we go to a website, that's encapsulation. It encapsulates, adds the headers all the way down so it encapsulates around the data, gets to the physical layer, and once it gets to the physical layer, the ones and zeroes, it goes to the destination. What do you think happens at the other side?

Demultiplexing

- Performed by the receiving machine
- Reverses the encapsulation process

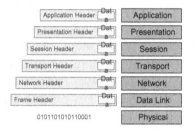

Demultiplexing. Somebody will probably say decapsulation; no, unfortunately, it's demultiplexing. Demultiplexing is actually the reverse of encapsulation. Decapsulation would have probably sounded better but its demultiplexing.

Now I take my ones and zeroes at the physical layer, they go up to the data link layer, and they slap the frame header on. And then it goes up to the network layer, so I have the network. They're actually doing what? They're taking the headers off. When it gets there and it comes up, it gets the entire frame. Remember, the frame header represents all of the headers from encapsulation. If you look at the actual encapsulation diagram, you see all the headers are there for the seven layers of OSI model. When the frame data are created, it starts stripping the headers off until it gets back to the application at the layer of the person reading your email or of the website reading your query to the website, and that's the process. So as I said, it goes down the stack, which is encapsulation; then, the receiving machine reverses the encapsulation process and does demultiplexing. And that's the process of how the data flow between a client and server machine.

So every day you're on your computer and you're doing anything on your phones today, in the same way, you're at the application layer. All this other stuff is taking place underneath. Now you can start thinking about this: If you have the choice whether to work at the top or work at the lowest layer and understand the bits and bytes, where would you work? You understand the lowest layer. Because anybody can understand the top layer. We all know how it works on a computer. We get on, we start clicking on buttons and figuring out the application layer. When you get into Microsoft Word, you get into Office, you get into Google Chrome. And again, with any of these things it's a little bit of a learning curve as we click around. We just click around to figure what works and doesn't work. While we're doing that, underneath all that is entire stuff taking place in the other layers. You have to understand what is taking place in the other layers if you want to be either a hacker or if you want to just understand hacking and be an expert in security consulting.

TCP/IP

- TCP/IP is a condensed version of the OSI Model
  ○ Throughout this book, we will use the OSI Model

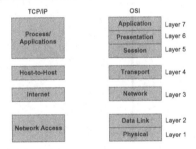

OSI = Open Systems Interconnection

The OSI layer, the OSI model that we have been talking about, that is the seven-layer model. We have another model that is a little bit more recognized when it comes to military DOD, Department of Defense, those types of things. That's the TCP/IP layered model. And the TCP/IP model combines layer 5, 6, and 7 of the OSI model. That is the application, presentation, and the session layer is combined into one layer called the application layer. And the transport layer is called host to host in some models. The network layer is called the Internet, and then the network access layers are a combination that they link in the physical. Now, a lot of people will reference the TCP/IP model, but in the book, we're going to talk more about the OSI model.

We want to make sure we can maintain and understand throughout what happens at each layer. So let's talk a little bit about that here. We've got the physical layer. The physical layers, as I have already said, are the binary, the bits and the bytes, and the ones and the zeroes. The data link layer is the MAC address; that is the physical address of the network card. The network layer is the IP address, and that is where your routing takes place. So if you're in the same network, of course you don't have a routing table. If you're on a different network, you're going to have a routing table to know where to go to get to the other side. And then the transport layer is where we run our TCP or UDP—Transmission Control Protocol or User Datagram Protocol—those are the main protocols in the transport layer, which, as you might have gathered, are ports. There are ports located there in the transport layer because that identifies the port. And then we already talk about the session presentation application. That's the main seven layers of the OSI model.

Flow of Data

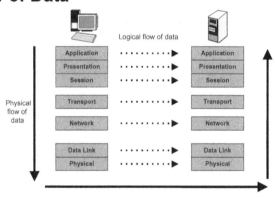

So how do the data flow? Logically, whatever happens to the application of the sender happens in the reverse in the multiplex and when it gets to the top of the OSI model, it's back to the normal form it was sent down in the OSI model by the sending machine. The physical flow of data, therefore, goes down the OSI layers. So when you hit send, it goes down to the application presentation session, the transport network data link, and turns into ones and zeroes. Once it turns into ones and zeroes, it gets transmitted across the median to the other machine; the ones and zeroes are passed up to the physical layer and then we go to the process. It is demultiplexed until it matches what happened in the application layer of the sender. The key here is, as the diagram shows, the logical flow of the data application layer, the presentation—whatever layer you're at—that same process happens in reverse on the other side. As we send it down or encapsulate it, we're adding headers on to the existing information and when we get it to the other side and we demultiplexed it, we're stripping those headers off until what remains is the application header with the data.

Devices Within the OSI Model

- Switches and routers are the cornerstone for access control
- A switch is used to connect multiple machines within a network
  - This connection takes place at Layer 2 (Data Link)
- A router is used to connect multiple networks throughout the enterprise
  - The router connection is carried out at Layer 3 (Network)

How do we do it? We've got to connect the devices. We can't just put two devices together with a wire;—well, you can, but then that's never a good network. If it's the only thing you have, you have two devices connected by a network cable. That's not going to get you very far in this world. So what we do is actually do switches and routers to connect multiple machines with the network. What we do is that layer 2, the data link layer with the switch traditionally. We're talking about traditional switches. You hear some people say layer 3, layer 4, layer 7 switches, but for now we'll just deal with switches in the traditional form. They are a layer 2 device. The switch doesn't handle the actual routing; a switch actually does the MAC addresses. So the switch sends traffic between the normal subnet and the same network. You use a router when you want to connect multiple networks throughout the enterprise.

As I said, you can do layer 3 routing on a switch but again we're going into a more traditional sense, and that traditional sense is a router that usually connects multiple networks throughout the enterprise, which is layer 3. So a router operates at layer 3 and a switch operates at layer 2 because it provides us our MAC address. Remember, layer 2 is the data link layer, while layer 3 is the network layer. Then what we do is we connect all our machines with these switches and routers, and that's how we get our large networks in our enterprise.

Switch Connecting Two Machines

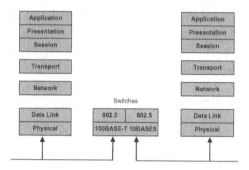

Here's an example of a traditional switch with two machines. The sender machine will send the application, and it will encapsulate all the way down to the physical layer to ones and zeroes and then in this diagram, it's showing a switch. The switch comes in play at layer 2. So this is a layer 2 switch, and the data come up to the switch, the switch looks at that and says, "Where's the MAC address of this machine?" and sends it off to the appropriate address of the machine. As you're going through your studies and you're doing research, remember that all data are delivered to the MAC address. Another way of saying that is no data is delivered until the MAC physical address is identified, so all data are delivered to the MAC address.

Router Connecting Two Networks

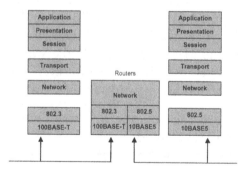

The routers operate at layer 3. When a switch is the same network device as the IP address structure, the same as the other, then we use virtual LANs versus lands and we won't get into that right now. What happens is now the data, when it's encapsulated, go down to the wire, ones and zeroes. The ones and zeroes are passed through this device, a network device, which means it can connect more than one network together. So the router is a routing device between multiple networks that are on different addresses, and that's how we actually do everything. So routing takes place at layer 3.

Layer 2, the data link layer, is where your data are delivered to the MAC address and routing, which gets you to the subnet to allow layer 2 to take over. So that's the best way to think about all of this. A layer 3 device will get you to the layer 3 device that is responsible for the network that you are searching for. Once you get there, it will do an ARP, Address Resolution Protocol, which again is more stuff that we will continue to talk about here. ARP takes the IP address and says this is the physical address or the IP Address. We'll look at some examples of that in diagrams as we continue.

CHAPTER 3

Analyzed Traffic

Analyzing Traffic With Protocol Analyzers

- The most effective method to analyze network traffic is to use a tool
- A number of protocol analysis tools are available:
  - Wireshark
  - Iris
  - Sniffer
- Wireshark is a free, open-source tool that has the capability to display network traffic in a Graphical User Interface (GUI)
- Features of Wireshark include
  - Ability to decode traffic on the fly
  - Ability to reconstruct sessions
  - Ability to analyze virtually any protocol
- Download Wireshark at www.wireshark.org

The key to all is you've got to be able to analyze network traffic. Now we're going to do protocol analysis; a whole chapter of it is coming up. But I want to talk about what protocol analysis is. Protocol analysis is basically looking at the packets at the lowest level, which is the packet level. We have a saying out in the industry: The packets do not lie. They may be encrypted and hide information, but the packets do not lie. So unless somebody has encrypted the data or is making it harder for you with what we call one of those techniques, when you read the packets, they're going to tell you the story of what's taking place on the network. In most cases, what's taking place as far as the incident, if you're doing an incident response or an investigation, those types of things. It's very important that we remember that packets do not lie, so we always look at the packets. Once we look at the packets, we're usually in pretty good shape for that.

One of the most popular tools for doing this is a tool called Wireshark. It's a free open-sourced tool that is excellent at decoding different types of network protocols and traffics. It's a very powerful tool and I highly recommend that you check it out. The good news is that it's free. We don't always get good free tools, but in this case,

Wireshark is free and good. And if you really want to be doing this stuff and be good at this stuff, you need to learn protocol analysis, and one of the best tools for doing that is Wireshark. The one downside of Wireshark is it doesn't have the capability of replay packets, like when you take a packet capture and peek at the app library with the way the packets are saved. If you take that and you try to actually replay, you've got to use a third-party tool. Wireshark doesn't give us that capability.

IPv4 Header

0		16	32

Version	Internet Header Length (IHL)	Type of Service (TOS)	Total Length (TL)
Identification		Flags	Fragment Offset
Time to Live (TTL)	Protocol	Header Checksum	
Source IP Address			
Destination IP Address			
Options			

This is what the IPv4 header looks like. You've got the version, the header length, and the type of service. This diagram shows you the IPv4 header. The most important thing to remember about the IPv4 header is that everything that is carried in IP—Internet Protocol—TCP, UDP, whatever it is, is encapsulated or contained within IP. Remember we talked about how encapsulation is the process of putting things inside of things. That's exactly what the IPv4 header does. It actually takes the protocol, whatever protocol is in there, and it encapsulates it inside of that. So you have the IPv4 header and then you'll have another header that will be the encapsulated protocol.

We'll look at those different things. One of the most important things to remember is on the IPv4 version, it's a four there and the header length will be a five. And we'll get into, in a little while, why that header length is a five. But as you look at the diagram you will see there are five levels in the diagram. That is where the five comes from, and that is what we call five 32-bit words. We'll cover more of that as well as look at an actual screenshot of a packet capture.

IPv4 Header (cont)

- Version
  - Identifies version of IP that generated the datagram
- IHL
  - Specifies the length of the header in 32-bit words
  - Normally 5 = (532-bit words = 20 bytes)
- TOS
  - Designed to carry information for QoS
- TL
  - Specifies the total length of the IP datagram
  - Maximum length is 65,535 (16 bits)
- TTL
  - Length of time the datagram will live on network
- Protocol
  - 6 = TCP, 17 = UDP

As I said, the IPv4 header version, header links five 32 bit words, which is 20 bytes, 160 bits; that's where it all comes from. And then, you have the time to live (TTL); the time that the datagram will be live on the network, and we have the protocol. The IP type 6 is TCP. IP type 17 is UDP. These are decimal numbers. IP Protocol type 1 is ICMP. These are important to know, especially if you want to take any type of certification examinations. They will ask all these different ICMP types, those types of things. It's important to know because we can look at an IP packet and we have to see the encapsulated protocol to know what it is. We can actually read the IP protocol type field to know what's carried within the packet without drilling down further into the packet to find that information, which is quite a powerful thing.

IPv4 Address Classes

- Class A

0	7 bits Net ID	24 bits Host ID

- Class B

1	0	14 bits Net ID	16 bits Host ID

- Class C

1	1	0	21 bits Net ID	8 bits HostID

Just a quick thing here on addressing: Most of you probably have heard of Class A address, Class B address, and Class C address. That's probably one of the most misunderstood things I've come across. This is all the IPv4 addressing. We call this 32-bit notation. And it's 32-bit notation because it's represented as four 8 bits separated by dot. So it's really binary, ones and zeroes, live everything else. And what we do is take that first 8 bits, and we use that to identify what's going to be our class of network. If the first 8 bits is a zero, if it starts with a zero, it's a class A network and that's because of our binary. Seven bits of binary can add up to a certain number. Now, we'd give you that number, but I'll leave it to you for homework. It's not hard to figure out because if 8 bits is 0 to 255 or maximum number of 255, 256 total, what's seven bits? Yeah, I think some of you probably got the answer already and we'll leave that to you.

Class B is in the diagram. If you look at Class B, it starts with a one followed by a zero because that is saying I got a one, which means that's the 8 bit. If you do your binary in your head like some people do, you can see it's easy to do; just in your thinking you can say 2 to the 0 is one. 2 to the 2 or 2 squared is 4. Two to the 0 is one, 2 to the 1 is 2, 2 squared is 4, 2 cubed is 8, 2 to the 4 is 16. You get the idea. So you just count up 8 bits, always starting with zero. A lot of people make the mistake of 8 bits starting with zero. So if we go with 8 bits with zero, we go 1, 2, 4, 8, 16, 32, 64, and 128. That one being there says, "Class B address starts at 128. Now it says zero in the next column, so that means it goes 128 up to—what's 128 plus 64? When you add 128 plus 64, you get 192. So that means Class B is 128 up to 191, all right? That is Class B. Class C starts at 192 and goes up. And you see that because in your 8 bits of the first of the dotted octet, you have a one and a one. 128 plus 64, which is those two-bit positions because they're 2 to the 6th and 2 to the 7th, respectively. 128 plus 64 equals 192; therefore, the Class C addresses start at 192." That's how you tell it and that's how it looks.

A lot of people are saying, "Okay, well, Class A is 24 bit of host, 8 bits a network," and that's true. Class B is 16 bits of host, 16 bits of network, and Class C is 24 bits of host and only 8 bits of network. It doesn't matter how you really want to say it or look at it; just understand that the classing of the address is identified by the first two bits in the first dotted octet. The zero start, meaning it's a Class A, goes from 0 to 127. Class B, from 128 to 191; and Class C, from 192, if you're going to say 256, you're going to be wrong because we start multicast at 224. Class C goes from 191 to 223. And again, that is IPv4 addressing, which if most people get their way will go away eventually.

IPv4 Address Classes (cont)

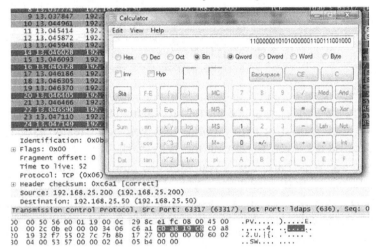

So here are the IP address classes. This is the different thing in the address classes. When you look at the IP address classes, you see it's all binary; that's the binary word of this IP address. And as we look at the diagram here that shows the calculator for the IP address the Q word, the Quad word, you can see in the actual highlighted area are C0A819C8, and that's the IP address. So what is C0? Well, if you go do your hexadecimal and you remember 0 is 16th to the zero with 0×16 is 00 and C is times 16th to the 1st. Well, C is $\times 16$, so what is C? In hexadecimal, you go 0, 1, 2, 3, 4, 5, 6, 7, 8, 9. A is 10, B is 11, and C is 12. What is 12×16? 192. So that's where the address comes from. That address is 192. That's how you figure these things out. You go into the hexadecimal and you calculate it, and as I said, it's dotted octet, or 8 bits per number. When you look at that, you'll see there are four different series of hexadecimal digits, and that is because in hexadecimal, two digits of hexadecimal is 8 bits, and that's where it comes from.

IPv4 Addresses (cont)

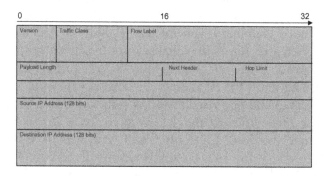

There is another diagram showing the same type of thing. You can actually get practice in how to calculate these if you don't see it in the tool. You'd probably notice that you don't really have to calculate because it's given to you by the Wireshark. If you look at the diagram, you see Wireshark shows you what the actual source and destination IP address of that packet is so you don't have to calculate it. But this is what we call a GUI or higher level protocol analysis tool, and we do have some low-level protocol analysis tools that will not give you this answer that easily.

IPv6 Header

0		16		32
Version	Traffic Class	Flow Label		
Payload Length			Next Header	Hop Limit
Source IP Address (128 bits)				
Destination IP Address (128 bits)				

Here we want to talk about IPv6. IPv6 went from 32 bits of addressing, which is IPv4, and decided they were going to do 128 bits of addressing. So now, we've got a 128-bit source address, 128-bit destination address. As you look in the diagram at the IPv6 header, you can see it's the same format and very similar to the IPv4 header. We've got the version number, but instead of the header link, you have the traffic class. The version number in IPv4 was 4 and the version number on IPv6, is 6—hey, good guess. Traffic class is how we do QoS, or Quality

Of Service, those types of things. That gives you an idea of how the IPv6 header looks. A controversial topic, it is usually stuff like that. I tell the people I was actually doing IPv6 training in the year 2000. Yes, folks, since the year 2000, we've been trying to get people to adapt IPv6, and the military, the American US Department of Defense, has had numerous deadlines come up where they said their networks will be fully up IPv6 compatible and working. To this day, they are not fully up to IPv6 compatible and working. So this is probably going to be a while still.

IPv6 Header (cont

- Version
  - Identifies version of IP that generated the datagram
- Traffic Class
  - 8-bit field for marking desired QoS
- Flow Label
  - 20-bit label for data flow
- Payload Length
  - 16-bit length of the payload
- Next Header
  - Identify the type of header following the IPv6 header
- Hop Limit
  - Similar to TTL in IPv4

And as I said, Traffic class is that 8-bit field for marking the desired quality of service. Flow label tells you the flow of data. Payload link is the 16-bit link. Next, header is the type of header followed by the IPv6 header. And Hop Limit is where we have analogy, it's an analogy to the time to live in IPv4.

IPv6 Address

- 128 bits

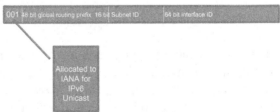

This is what the addressing looks like. We have a 128 bit, so we actually have what's called a 48-bit global routing prefix, followed by a 16-bit subnet ID and a 64-bit interface ID. So that's what it looks like and, as you're thinking and reading this is you can probably imagine when we go from reading 32 bits to try to read 128 bits, that can be a bit of a challenge.

IPv6 Addresses

```
Wireless LAN adapter Wireless Network Connection:

   Connection-specific DNS Suffix  . : globalsuite.net
   Description . . . . . . . . . . . : Dell Wireless 1505 Draft 802.11n WLAN M
i-Card
   Physical Address. . . . . . . . . : 00-1E-4C-63-DC-A2
   DHCP Enabled. . . . . . . . . . . : Yes
   Autoconfiguration Enabled . . . . : Yes
   IPv6 Address. . . . . . . . . . . : 2002:c612:98e3:a:a8dd:3c6a:92e:7d2e(Pre
rred)
   Site-local IPv6 Address . . . . . : fec0::a:a8dd:3c6a:92e:7d2e%2(Preferred)
   Temporary IPv6 Address. . . . . . : 2002:c612:98e3:a:2565:dae7:1520:3e65(Pr
erred)
   Link-local IPv6 Address . . . . . : fe80::a8dd:3c6a:92e:7d2e%10(Preferred)
   IPv4 Address. . . . . . . . . . . : 198.18.152.227(Preferred)
   Subnet Mask . . . . . . . . . . . : 255.255.0.0
   Lease Obtained. . . . . . . . . . : Sunday, December 20, 2009 10:28:20 AM
   Lease Expires . . . . . . . . . . : Monday, December 21, 2009 12:01:37 PM
   Default Gateway . . . . . . . . . : 198.18.0.1
   DHCP Server . . . . . . . . . . . : 198.18.0.1
   DHCPv6 IAID . . . . . . . . . . . : 167779916
   DNS Servers . . . . . . . . . . . : 4.2.2.1
   NetBIOS over Tcpip. . . . . . . . : Enabled
```

This is the actual look of an IPv6 address here in this diagram. If you look at the diagram, you can see we have FEC0, those types of things, and then we got colon, colon. But what happens is in IPv6 you're going to have a lots of repeating zeroes because it is such a big number. So IPv6 allows you to use a colon to eliminate all those repeating zeroes.

IPv6 Addresses (cont)

What does all that mean? If you look at the next diagram, you can see our address in the middle window that is highlighted in blue that says FE80::A8DD::360. You get the idea. Now if you're down here into the bottom area, not the middle section as highlighted in a darker blue, you see there's your FE80. But wait a minute, we've got 6 or 12 zeroes before we get to A8DD. We look up here, and all we have are colons, so the colons represent repeated zeroes. That's how it actually looks when you use the shorthand to eliminate the repeated zeroes and that is how it would actually look on the wire with all those repeated zeroes. This is a human readable form, and this is more of a machine readable form, which is why it's down in the lower part of Wireshark, because it is hexadecimal.

UDP Header

0	16	32
Source Port	Destination Port	
Length	Checksum	
Data		

- 16-bit source and destination ports

Now we get to UDP. IP, remember, encapsulates all protocols. The UDP header is kind of sparse. When you look at the UDP header, if you look at the diagram, and you look at the UDP header, you see the UDP header doesn't consist of whole lot of stuff. Why is that? Speed. Remember, UDP was used for speed. User data was mainly for speed. They didn't want to wait for data so what they did is they put in a very lightweight header so it's got a source port, it's got a destination port, it's got link, it's got text, it's got data, and that's it. That's all you have in UDP header and that is why it's so fast as it doesn't have to set up all this other stuff. But remember, it still encapsulated to contain within the IP header. Go to the IP header and look at the IP protocol type. Does anybody remember what the IP protocol type for UDP was? 17. If I look at hexadecimal, I can't see a number 167, so instead I am going to see in a 11.

TCP Header

0		16						32
Source Port		Destination Port						
Sequence Number								
Acknowledgement Number								
Hdr Lgth	Reserved	U	A	P	R	S	F	Window Size
Checksum		Urgent Pointer						
Options								

And here is the main workhorse, the TCP header. The TCP header, when you look at it, has a lot more stuff. That's because we have to guarantee our reliability and guarantee delivery. So since we've got to guarantee delivery, you've got a source port, you've got a destination port, you've got a sequence number, you've got an Acknowledgment Number, you've got a header link, and you've got what we call the flags. Most important probably for hackers and for security people, is to understand these flags. You want to understand these flags as much as you know the alphabet.

If you look at these flags in that diagram you see U, A, P, R, S, F. U is for urgent, A is for ACK, P is for Push, R is for Reset, S is for Synchronize, and F is for Finish. We'll cover each one of these flags momentarily. But there is no real easy way to remember these. We've got mnemonics for the OSI model. All people seem to need data processing and please do not throw sausage pizza away. And now here, we do here. We have "unskilled attackers pester real security folk." So, again, "unskilled attackers pester real security folk." That's a nice little acronym for the flags. But I just remember them as U, A, P, R, S, F.

TCP Header Composition

- Source and Destination ports: 16 bits
- Sequence and Acknowledgement numbers: 32 bits
- Flags:
  - URG
  - ACK
  - PSH
  - RST
  - SYN
  - FIN
- Window Size: 16 bits

Here's what it means. We've got a sequence and acknowledgment numbers which are 32 bits in size. That means there are four billion possible combinations. And then we have what's called the flags. The flags tell us what's taking place in the packet. We have the urgent flag, and the urgent flag means I've got data that I request you do not buffer. Remember, the receiving station knows its network better than anybody else, so it might ignore whatever the header tells it. In this case, urgent data means, "do not buffer, send my data directly into memory," which in most cases is a stack. The ACK is acknowledged. I am acknowledging something you sent.

A very important flag for us in hacking, and even more so in internet response and forensics, is the Push, PSH, the push flag. The push flag means I have data in the packet. You can imagine that if the push flags mean I have data in the packet, if I am compromising somebody's data, what's going to be set is the push flag, exactly. Since the push flag is going to be set, we like to look for push flags to see what's taking place on the network because that's when the data is going to fly. That password they cracked or whatever they cracked will have push flags in their data.

Then the reset. The reset is what we call the abnormal close. The reset is an abnormal close because something is going on, something is going wrong with our network and in TCP the logic is, if I don't send something or if you send me something I didn't request, I am going to send a reset. Because a reset will tear down the connection and doing so allows the continuation on whatever the actual machine was trying to do. So we just reset it and we're done with it and we don't have to deal any more.

Synchronize is the first sequence of all TCP traffic, what we call the three-way handshake. The synchronize opens a connection with me. That's what a synchronize means. Please open a connection with me. Fin or finish is a normal close. When you look at that always remember that it is a normal close and that's the normal packets.

Now start thinking about what we call the hackers or the enemy. "Know your enemy," right? That's a famous saying. Hackers, your enemy, are going to do things to deviate from this norm. what we just discussed here is the normal and hackers pride themselves on doing something that is not normal. That is why hacker defenders are becoming security consultants or whatever, and we have to understand what's normal and what's not normal as well.

Viewing TCP/IP Headers

Now we have a nice little Wireshark capture here for you in this diagram. You see it's been sorted on TCP. So in the top window, it's on number 3333. That 3333 is the actual packet. We see the flags that are set and we'll expand more on that later. But what I want you to look at starts with a frame followed by the Ethernet and then you have IP, Internet Protocol. The IP header is always the first header of the frame after the actual frame itself. So now when you look at it, you see V4 so IPv4, header link is 20 bytes, and again that's because of five 32 bit words, which means 160 bits. That's where all that comes from. When you start looking, you see we've got the time to live. We explained what the time to live was, how long the packet is going to actually live in the actual network. And then we've got the protocol. And the protocol is IP protocol type 6. IP Protocol type 6, as we've said earlier, is TCP. The source address, destination address, and then time for the encapsulated protocol. In this case, we have the encapsulated protocol as TCP, Transmission Control Protocol. When you look at that now, we know this is going to be equivalent to what we looked at in that TCP header. There is going to be a lot of data here that we have to take into account. When you look at the flag, and we'll cover these momentarily, those are the flags that were set in this packet.

It is all in the Packet!

- Observe the packet capture below
- What is wrong here?

```
Flags: 0x29 (FIN, PSH, URG)
    0... .... = Congestion Window Reduced (CWR): Not set
    .0.. .... = ECN-Echo: Not set
    ..1. .... = Urgent: Set
    ...0 .... = Acknowledgment: Not set
    .... 1... = Push: Set
    .... .0.. = Reset: Not set
    .... ..0. = Syn: Not set
    .... ...1 = Fin: Set
```

Now when you look at this next diagram, look at that packet capture, and what is wrong with that packet capture? The thing is when you look at a packet capture, you want to see the flags. If it's TCP traffic, go look at the flags because, what flag did we say was the one that would identify data? That's right, the push flag. So if you actually look at the push flag, what that means is there are data in the packet. But in this case, it's set. We see fin is set, which is finish, which is a normal close of a connection. We see push, which is data, is set so there is data in the packet, and then we see urgent, which means don't buffer my data.

So let's think about this logically for a second. If a FIN flag is set and that is a normal close, is it normal to close, send the packet that says close my connection, and include data in the packet too? I would say it's not normal. And in this case you can't send a FIN packet with a push flag or an urgent flag set. This is what's known as the Christmas tree attack or the x-mas scan. The Christmas tree attack is usually traditionally setting all six flags. The signature of in map, network mapper, a well-known port mapping tool for the hacking side and security side as well, it's a great tool. The actual process here is Fin Push, and urgent is a Christmas tree scan. So rather than set all six flags in map sets FIN, push, and urgent and that is what you're seeing here in that diagram.

TCP flags under the hood

URG	ACK	PSH	RST	SYN	FIN
Bit 5	Bit 4	Bit 3	Bit 2	Bit 1	Bit 0
32	16	8	4	2	1

When you look at this next diagram, it's a table to show you how this works. It's binary. Remember, everything is binary and we explained that to you: urgent, ACK, push, reset, SYN and FIN or unskilled attackers pester real security folk. And we did this because we want you to understand since it's bits of binary. What that means is the flag is set. So we had the FIN flag set, the push flag set, and the urgent flag set. That means the binary bit position of the zero, the two to the zero, two to the third and two to the fifth. So, the decimal number for that would be 32 plus 8 plus 1 or 41.

What would be the hexadecimal number? You can do it a dozen different ways; it doesn't matter, whatever works for you. Pull out your Windows calculator if you have to, but it's pretty easy to look at. 41 goes into 32 goes into 41, how many times? 16 goes into 41 how many times. What's 2×16? 32. What's 41 minus 32? 9. A 2 and a 9. So, the hexadecimal value of—a decimal value of 41 is 29. If you look at our previous diagram, you'll see this is correct. The flag is FIN, push and urgent do indeed add up to hex 29.

What Is a Threat?

- Any event that has the potential to cause harm to information or an information system
- An important part of developing an access-control solution is understanding the nature of the threat

What exactly is a threat? This is what it's all about with hacking and what it's all about with our security. We have to look at our threats. I think everybody reading this understands there is not any possibility that we're going to have perfect security. One, we wouldn't have a job, but I think our jobs are pretty safe for a long time because perfect security is a long way from happening. Perfect security would be nothing's allowed, a paranoid approach. We know we can't do a paranoid approach because if we do a paranoid approach, it's not going to work.

So what we do is Threat analysis. When you're setting up your security architecture, you want to know what the threat is. Are you an entity that's going to have a government or a nation state-backed threat? If you are, that's a huge part of your security. Because you're going to have nation states and adversaries going against you. And there's a well-known saying, and it's quite probably true for the most part, "If a deliberate attacker with unlimited resources think NSA state government here wants to target you, they're probably going to break in." We're not talking defense right now, but in one of the series, we will talk defense and when we talk defense, we're going to explain how we leverage that and accept the reality that there is no perfect security, but we can come pretty darn gone close and that is part of defense.

When you think about your access and control and how you're going to protect your network and stuff like that, it is understanding the nature of the threat. For our security consultancy and for our hacking, but especially for security consulting, if you want to be a security consultant, the better you can explain the threat to clients, the better you can justify that they need the solution you are trying to present for them.

Know Your Adversary

- Script kiddies
  - Little to no knowledge of networks
  - Dangerous because of the sophistication of the tools
    - ☐ Exploit frameworks
- Professional hackers
  - No longer the kid in the basement
  - Crime links
  - Nation state backing

We've got what we call these adversaries and there are a lot of different categories out there. We won't spend too much time on the categories for adversaries. Just understand the script kiddie. We love to call them script kiddie because they pretty much have no knowledge of networks and they don't know a whole lot of things. The problem with the script kiddie is the sophistication of the tools. There's an entire exploit framework out there that is basically point and click. In fact, one of the most famous hacks against the US Department of Defense, which I won't get into too much here in this mini book, was called Solar Sunrise. Solar Sunrise was being investigated and was considered to be nation state-backed, with a lot of government entities working on the attack. To make the long story short, they had broken into the offices of the Secretary of Defense's computer, OSD.mil. Well, come to find out, after all these agents did all this investigation, it was two teenage kids in Culver City, California. Yes, they had 30 agents doing investigations and it was two kids that ran a tool from the internet. And that's the key to all this. The sophistication of the tools has made it so much easier for script kiddies to do a lot of damage.

And then you've got the professional hackers. This is not the person that lives in their mom's basement and those types of things any more. Nowadays, it's big business, it's a lot of money, financial revenue, identity theft, all those types of things. It's no longer the kid in the basement. There's crime links, there's nation states, all those types of things.

Threat Containment

- Limiting the impact of a successful breach
- We know that an attacker might get in
  - There will always be vulnerabilities in systems and networks
    Code is very complex
    - Windows: 30–50 million Lines Of Code (LOC)
    - Cell phones: approaching 20 million LOC
    - Automobiles: => 2 million LOC
  - There always will be someone who has the information to write exploits and leverage vulnerabilities
    - Full-disclosure communities and the hacking underground
- With proper security controls, we can limit their capabilities once in

So what do we do? Well, you have to understand in security, the key is to limit the impact of a successful breach. There's always a chance that an attacker is going to get in; this is because your Windows code—not only Windows code but also all your code—is becoming more and more complex. And the more and more complex it becomes, the more and more bugs it will have. Because when you look at Windows traditionally, I think the last word on Windows 8 is there's 80 million lines of code. Cell phones are around 20 million lines of code. Automobiles, two million lines of code, and we had several big news stories on how hackers hacked into several different automobiles.

Because of this, there's always going to be bugs. This is why we're always going to have the different types of things. What we do from our hacking and security consultant perspective is to go look at sites to talk about these bugs, these vulnerabilities and exploits. And there are two types of disclosure. We talk about responsible disclosure and full disclosure. Responsible disclosure is, "I am going to tell you you've got a bug and I am going to give time to fix it." Full disclosure is, "Screw you, I am going to just release it and you live with what you want." And the problem is, no matter what side of the fence you are on, if you think full disclosure is good or responsible disclosure is good, somebody out there will always have the information and release it, all right? So that's the main thing to understand about threat containment. Again, we have to analyze the threat and our security is all about neutralizing that threat, and that is why we start with the foundation of understanding what is happening on our network. And we do that at the level of the packets, and that's why we started this series off with understanding TCP/IP 101.

Physical and Data Link

- Responsible for connecting the host to the network
- Contain the Media Access Control (MAC) Address
  - Can identify the physical machine in an
- The lowest level of data
  - Bits!

```
C:\>arp -a
Interface: 192.168.1.84 --- 0xa
  Internet Address      Physical Address      Type
  192.168.1.1           00-18-f6-4f-79-52     dynamic
  192.168.1.100         00-1f-5b-d1-cb-95     dynamic
  224.0.0.22            01-00-5e-00-00-16     static
```

Let's look at each layer in a little bit more detail. Because to understand the actual attack, we've got to understand what takes place at the layer. We talked about the physical layer and the data link layer. The data link layer, as we said, is the media access control layer, and the physical layer is the bits. The way to view this is to open up a terminal window and type in or command prompt in Windows world type in ARP for Address Resolution Protocol—A. That will show you your ARP table. Now remember what happens is that a packet, when it goes down to the wire, goes to the router and says, "Mr. Router, I am here and I am going to this network, 192.168.20.0." And Mr. Router looks at it and says, "I am not 192.168.20.0. My neighbor is." And he looks at his routing table and says, "Who's my neighbor?" And she sends the packet off to his neighbor. Finally, when it gets to the router of the actual local area subnet, that router generates an ARP, Address Resolution Protocol, who has this IP Address. And that IP address gets responded to with a packet that says it's literally in the packets. When you look at the packets, it says, "Who has this address?" And it comes back and it says, "This address is at..." and tells you the MAC address or the Physical Access Control Access.

Network and Transport

- Responsible for routing information to its destination
  - Network
- Responsible for managing data delivery
  - Transport
- Common location for evidence of misuse
  - Hackers manipulate these layers often
    - ☐ IP address
    - ☐ Routing information
    - ☐ Packet structure

The network and transport layers. As we said, the routing information is layer 3. The transport layer is layer 4. Hackers are always manipulating these addresses; this is why it's important that you know this type of information. Because this is where they can manipulate the IP addresses, and the MAC addresses, and where they can manipulate the actual structure of the packet, and they can actually set up detours and change the routing structure of packets as well. Very powerful stuff.

Session

- Responsible for creating dialog between host connections
  - Establishing
  - Maintaining
  - Managing
- Remote procedure calls
  - SUN RPCs
  - NFS
  - Microsoft RPCs
    - ☐ nbtstat

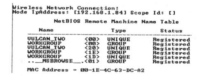

The session layer is your dialog between host connections. The best way to think about this is remote procedure calls.

If you look at the diagram, that diagram is showing you a picture of Nbtstat. What you can do is you can open a window because Microsoft's RPC, Remote Procedure Call, uses that NETBIOS traffic.

You can open up a command prompt window and type in Nbtstat/? question mark. And that will show you all the different options of Nbtstat. The one you want to look at is Nbtstat−A, then put in the IP address that you want to enumerate on what we call the NetBIOS machine table. When you look at that diagram, you see the NetBIOS machine name table actually gives you the name of the machine, the domain. In this case, you see the machine name is Vulcan 2, the domain is workgroup. That means it's never been part of a domain so this is a standalone machine; it's not part of a domain. If it's part of a domain it would have a domain name there instead of workgroup. This is powerful stuff we can do at the session layer.

NetBIOS Suffixes (16[th]Character)

Name	Number(h)	Type	Usage
<computername>	00	U	Workstation Service
<computername>	01	U	Messenger Service
_ _MSBROWSE_ _>	01	G	Master Browser
<computername>	03	U	Messenger Service
<computername>	06	U	RAS Server Service
<computername>	1F	U	NetDDE Service
<computername>	20	U	File Server Service
<computername>	21	U	RAS Client Service
<computername>	22	U	Microsoft Exchange Interchange (MSMail Connector)
<computername>	23	U	Microsoft Exchange Store
<computername>	24	U	Microsoft Exchange Directory
<computername>	30	U	Modem Sharing Server Service
<computername>	31	U	Modem Sharing Client Service
<computername>	43	U	SMS Clients Remote Control
<computername>	44	U	SMS Administrators Remote Control Tool
<computername>	45	U	SMS Clients Remote Chat
<computername>	46	U	SMS Clients Remote Transfer
<computername>	4C	U	DEC Pathworks TCPIP service on Windows NT
<computername>	42	U	McAfee anti-virus
<computername>	52	U	DEC Pathworks TCPIP service on Windows NT
<computername>	87	U	Microsoft Exchange MTA
<computername>	6A	U	Microsoft Exchange IMC
<computername>	BE	U	Network Monitor Agent
<computername>	BF	U	Network Monitor Application
<username>	03	U	Messenger Service
<domain>	00	G	Domain Name
<domain>	1B	U	Domain Master Browser
<domain>	1C	G	Domain Controllers
<domain>	1D	U	Master Browser
<domain>	1E	G	Browser Service Elections
<INet~Services>	1C	G	IIS
<IS~computer name>	00	U	IIS
<computername>	[2B]	U	Lotus Notes Server Service
IRISMULTICAST	[2F]	G	Lotus Notes
IRISNAMESERVER	[33]	G	Lotus Notes
Forte_$ND800ZA	[20]	U	DCA IrmaLan Gateway Server Service

In this table diagram that you're looking at, this is what we call the 16th byte or the 16th character on a Windows machine. The key you want to look at here are the domain ones. If you look at the number in the second column and you see the domain is 1C, that is, C as in Charlie, that's the domain controller. By doing that little Nbtstat drill we just talked about, where you open a command prompt and you do Nbtstat-A and then an IP address, if you get a 1C or 1Charlie return in that 16th byte address, which we showed you in the previous diagram, and you look at that and if that says 1C with the domain name, you now have a domain controller. Once you have a domain controller, you have identified the main actual computer probably on that network. And in most cases this is where the active directory and all the other stuff resides, which we call the keys to the kingdom for the hacker. So that's how you identify it. You just go do a simple Nbtstat which is part of NetBIOS statistics; that is what Windows actually likes to do, and that's how you identify it.

NetBIOS Registration Types

- U – Unique
  - Only one IP address allowed for that name
    - □ Name includes the 16thbyte!
- G – Group
  - Can have many IP addresses
- M - Multihomed
  - Name is unique
  - Allow up to 25 hosts to support multiple computers
- D – Domain
  - Support domains

These are your registration types. So when we are looking at those types of things, it's important to understand the U for Unique, only one IP address is allowed for that name. This is something you might have seen before. If you get on a Windows machine or you use virtualization and you do something, and it comes up and you get a duplicate name on the network, that duplicate name on the network is caused by this right here, registration. Because that name goes to register and says, "Wait a minute, I can't register, there's a unique name here already of XYZ." That's how we actually can identify duplicate names on the network. It doesn't give it to you for IP addresses, like a duplicate IP address does where it disables the IP protocol stat, but again it does give you quite a bit of information about the network.

Registered Domain Names

\\<domain_name>[00h]
This instance of the domain name is registered by the Workstation so that it can receive browser broadcasts from LAN Manager-based systems. This is the name to which server announcements are broadcast in Microsoft LAN Manager so that other Microsoft LAN Manager computers can track the servers on the network. Windows computers do not make these broadcasts unless the LMAnnounce option has been enabled by configuring the Server service in the Control Panel/Networks application.

\\<domain_name>[1Bh]
This instance of the domain name is registered by the Windows NT Server system that is running as the Domain Master Browser and is used to allow remote browsing of domains. When a WINS Server is queried for this name, a WINS Server returns the IP address of the system that registered this name.

\\<domain_name>[1Ch]
This name is registered for use by the domain controllers within the domain and can contain up to 25 IP addresses. One IP address will be that of the Primary Domain Controller (PDC) and the other 24 will be the IP addresses of Backup Domain Controllers (BDCs). The [1Ch] domain name is used by the BDCs to locate the PDC and is used when pass- through authentication is needed to validate a logon request.

\\<domain_name>[1Dh]
This instance of the domain name is registered only by the Master Browser, of which there can only be one for the domain. This name is used by the Backup Browsers to communicate with the Master Browser in order to retrieve the list of available servers from the Master Browser.

\\<domain_name>[1Eh]
This name is registered by all Browser servers and Potential Browser servers in a domain or workgroup. It is used for announcement requests which are sent by Master Browsers to fill up its browse lists, and for election request packets to force an election.

Registered domain names, there's just more information. Remember, the 1C is the domain controller so that shows and helps you do the domain controller.

Presentation

- Responsible for formatting and converting data for use by the computer
  - ASCII
  - EBCIDIC

The presentation layer is actually responsible for converting the data for use by the computer. This is where your character code set comes in. The typical character code set, probably everyone reading this is aware of, is A-S-C-I-I or ASCII, American Standard Code Information Interchange. But then you've got this thing called EBCIDIC, otherwise known as Extended Binary Coded Decimal Interchange Code. The presentation layer is where the formatting and converted data is, for use by the computer.

Application

- Interface between the users and the networks
- Most used layer
  - An evidence bonanza
- Significant traces of applications and activity
  - Many server services on clients
  - Logs
  - Processes
  - Network ports and connections

The application layer is the bonanza. That's where everything takes place. Think about it, everything you do, you sit in there and you do the application layer. That is how we do it. We always look at the application layer. We like the application layer, because that's easy. We just point and click and let the computer do all the work, right? That is where your server, your server sets, your clients, those types of things, that's where everything takes place. Your net reports and your connections. And that's pretty much the main components of TCP/IP 101, and this brings us to the end of our chapter.

CONCLUSION

So what do we do? We look at network protocols. Remember, with network protocols we had IP, the Internet Protocol, which is the main protocol that is used for all our network traffic. Within IP, Internet Protocol, we talked about two other protocols. We talked about TCP, Transmission Control Protocol, and UDP, User Datagram Protocol. What that means is TCP is guaranteed, and it means there's acknowledgment for the data. UDP is the connection list, no acknowledgment for the data. And then we looked at some packet headers and talked about IPV4 headers and IPV6 headers. We saw how IPV4 headers have a version number of 4, and IPV6 has a version number of 6. We saw how, in IPV6, if we display something in a GUI to read it, the trailing or the repeating zeroes are actually short-cut with colons. But when we look at it in hexadecimal, it continues and shows the actual repeated zeroes.

Remember, the IPV4 space is 32 bits, IPV6 is 128 bits. We have Class A, which starts with a zero, and we have Class B that starts with a 1, 1, 0 the first two bits. We also have Class C networks that starts with 1,1, and that's how we looked at it. And then we talked a little bit about traffic analysis and that was what takes place on the network. We said that the flags control, usually in TCP, is what's taking place on the network. So we looked at the six flags of TCP. We looked at urgent, act, push, reset, SYN, and FIN. And then we looked at a packet which was potentially crafted, and we discovered it had three flags set: the FIN, the push, and the urgent. That indeed was a crafted packet. And since it was a crafted packet, it was malicious and illegal on our network.